Primary Mathematics

1A

Level 1A (Textbook)

Tau Math
Education

COPYRIGHT & PUBLICATION INFORMATION

TAU Math – Primary Mathematics Level 1A Textbook

TAU Math is a mathematics-focused educational brand of Fliplecture, engaged in the publishing of mathematics textbooks and the delivery of related educational services.

Edition Information
First edition: 2026

Published by
TAU Math
(A brand of Fliplecture)

ISBN
978-93-5626-773-2

ACKNOWLEDGEMENTS

This book was developed through the collaborative efforts of a team of mathematics educators, academic professionals, and illustrators. Mathematics educators contributed to the structuring and sequencing of concepts, ensuring clarity and age-appropriate progression. Illustrators worked closely with the academic team to create visuals that support understanding and engagement.

We also acknowledge the contributions of teachers and academic reviewers who provided valuable feedback during the development process. Their insights helped refine the presentation and learning flow of the content.
We thank all individuals who contributed their time, expertise, and support to the creation of this textbook.

PREFACE

TAU Math is a comprehensive mathematics series designed to support learning across Primary Mathematics, Secondary Mathematics, and University Mathematics. The series provides a clear and continuous progression, guiding learners from foundational concepts to higher levels of mathematical thinking.

Each textbook is accompanied by a corresponding workbook, offering structured opportunities for practice, reinforcement, and consolidation. Together, they form an integrated learning system that supports guided instruction in classroom and tutoring environments.

The TAU Math series follows a carefully sequenced and structured mathematical progression, ensuring continuity, clarity, and steady skill development as learners advance through the levels.

Teachers and tutors are encouraged to introduce concepts through creative mathematics stories aligned with the lessons, helping learners connect ideas naturally and meaningfully. Practice and review activities are designed to strengthen skills, promote reasoning, and encourage learners to explain their thinking and develop confident problem-solving abilities.

Tau Math

Contents

Numbers 0 to 10

1.Counting

0
Zero

1
One

2
Two

3

Three

4

Four

5

Five

6

Six

7

Seven

8

Eight

9

Nine

10

Ten

1.Count and fill.

3

2.Find the Correct Set

(a) Which set shows 1

(b) Which set shows 7

(c) Which set shows 5

3.Find More, Fewer, or Equal.
Tick the correct picture.

(a) Which set has more?

(b) Which set has fewer?

(c) Look at the two sets. Are they equal? Tick Yes or No.

Yes   No

4. Count from 1 to 10

5.Count backward

6.What comes Next?

3	4	5	6		
1	2	3	4		

7.What comes before?

		6	7	8	9
		4	5	6	7

8.What comes in between?

1		3	4		6
5		7	8		10
2		4	7		9

9.Find the missing number.

1	2		4	
6	7			10
3		5		7

2

Ordinal Numbers

1 Order and Position

Children standing in a line to board the bus.

Ordinal numbers tell, who is **first**, **next**, and **last**.

1st is closest to the bus, and **8th** is the last in the line.

Understanding 1st, 2nd, Next To & Before

Learn positions in a line!

What is 1st

The 1st child is the one in front of everyone.

What is 2nd

The 2nd child is the one who stands after the first.

What is Next and Before

Two children are next to each other when they stand side by side.

A child is before another child when they are in front of them in the line.

1.Look at the picture of the train. Observe the position of each animal. Answer the questions below

(a) Which animal is in the 3rd carriage?

A. Dolphin B. Monkey C. Rabbit D. Cat

(b) Who is standing in the 5th place?

A. Rabbit B. Duck C. Bear D. Giraffe

(c) What is the ordinal position of the Giraffe?

A. 1st B. 2nd C. 4th D. 10th

(d) Which animal is in the last (10th) position?

A. Cat B. Deer C. Dog D. Elephant

(e) Who is right before the Dog?

A. Duck B. Cat C. Bear D. Rabbit

(f) Which animal is between Monkey and Rabbit?

A. Dolphin B. Elephant C. Dog D. Cat

(g) What is the 8th animal in the train?

A. Dog B. Cat C. Bear D. Sheep

(h) The Bear is in which position?

A. 7th B. 9th C. 3rd D. 10th

(i) Who is at the front of the train?

A. Elephant B. Giraffe C. Monkey D. Dolphin

(j) Which animal is next to the Dolphin?

A. Rabbit B. Giraffe C. Monkey D. Duck

Building Number Bonds

1 Number Bond Stories

There are **7 monkeys** in the jungle.

3 monkeys are playing on the vines.

4 monkeys are sitting on the ground.

Whole

7

4 3

Part Part

Make your own number bond stories:

8

5 3

5

3 2

1.Look at each picture. Write the correct part and whole numbers.

(a) Make Number Pair stories from the Playground

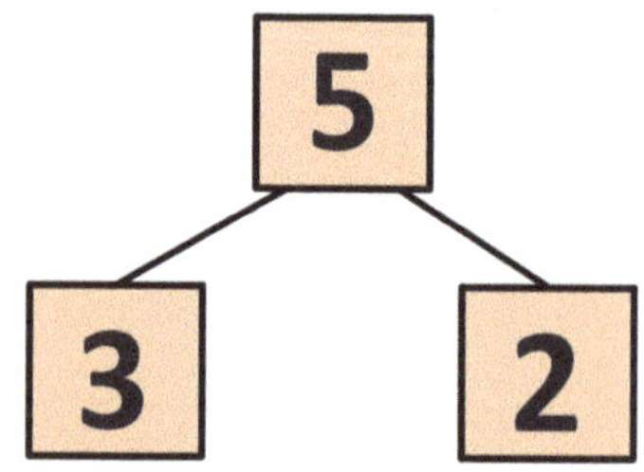

(b) List different ways to make 7

(c) How many fruits are inside and how many are outside?

(d) How many squirrels are above and how many are below?

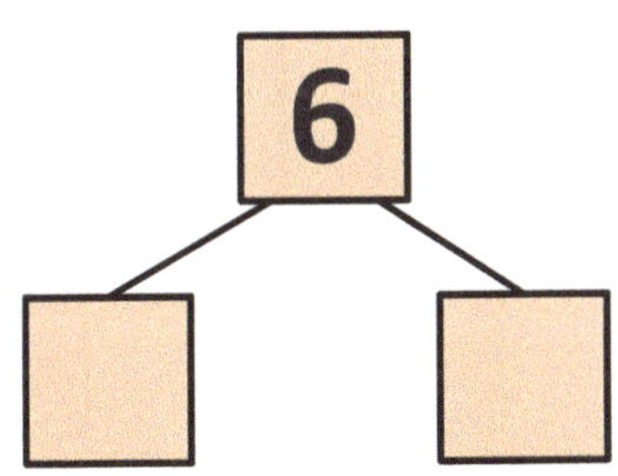

(e) Find all pairs of numbers that make 8.

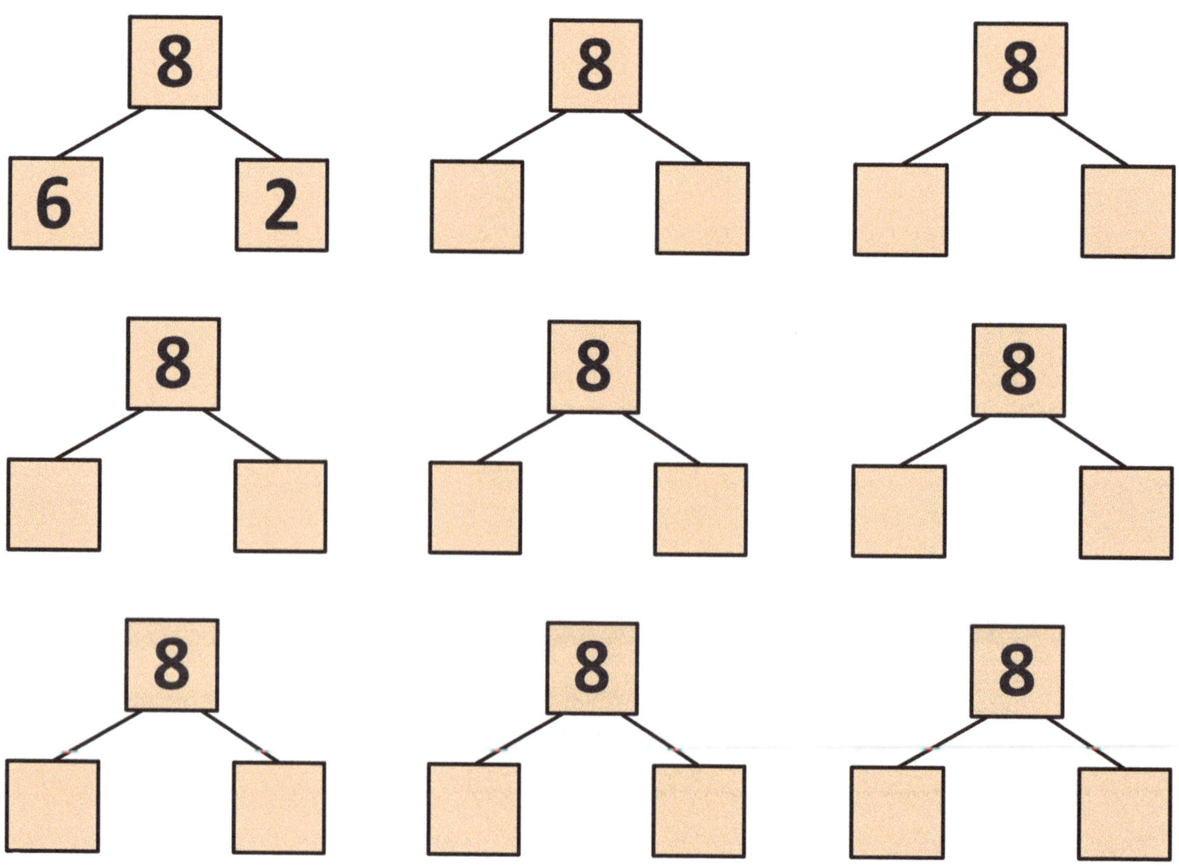

(f) Find all pairs of numbers that make 5.

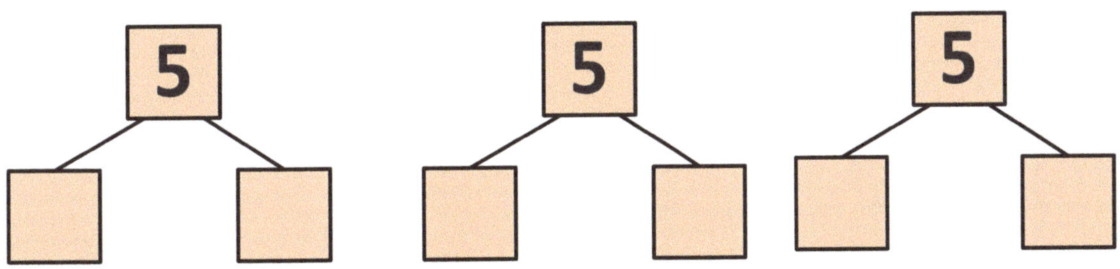

(g) Find the missing numbers?

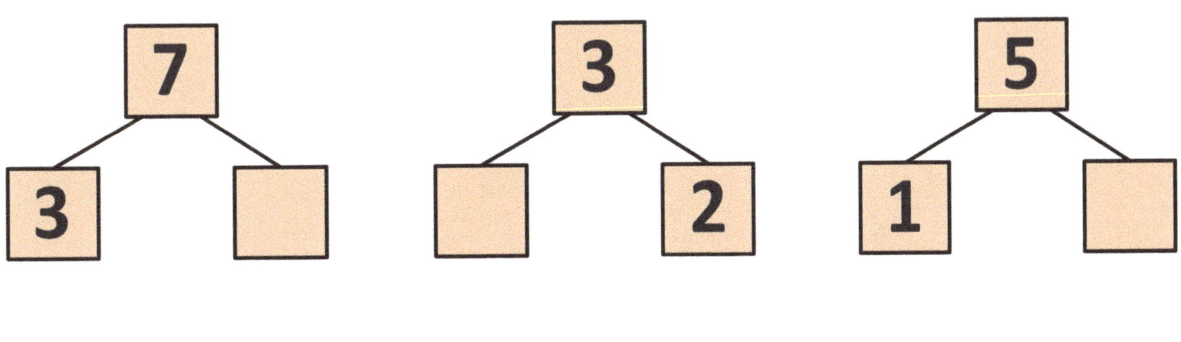

(h) Use the number cards to make number bonds for the given number.

5: 4, 1

8: 2, 6

2: ___, ___

7: ___, ___

4: ___, ___

9: ___, ___

6: ___, ___

3: ___, ___

10: ___, ___

(i) Look at the pictures below. Count the parts.

Fill in the two parts to make the number.

(1) ☐ and ☐ make ☐

(2) ☐ and ☐ make ☐

Addition Within 10

1 Learn Addition with Fun Picture Stories!

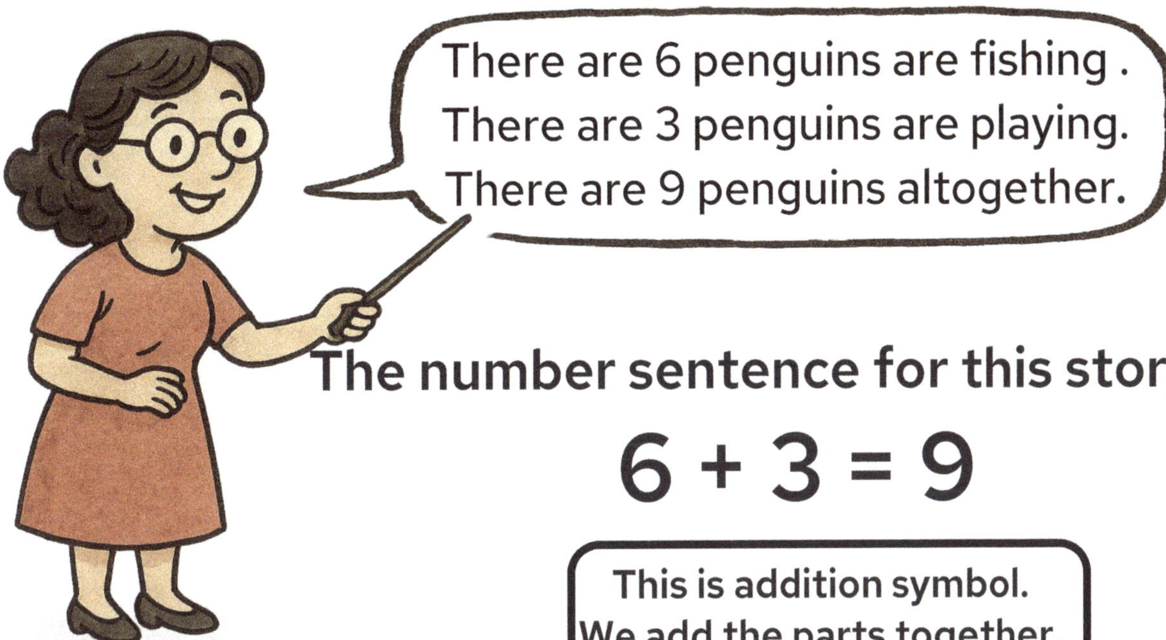

The number sentence for this story is:

$$6 + 3 = 9$$

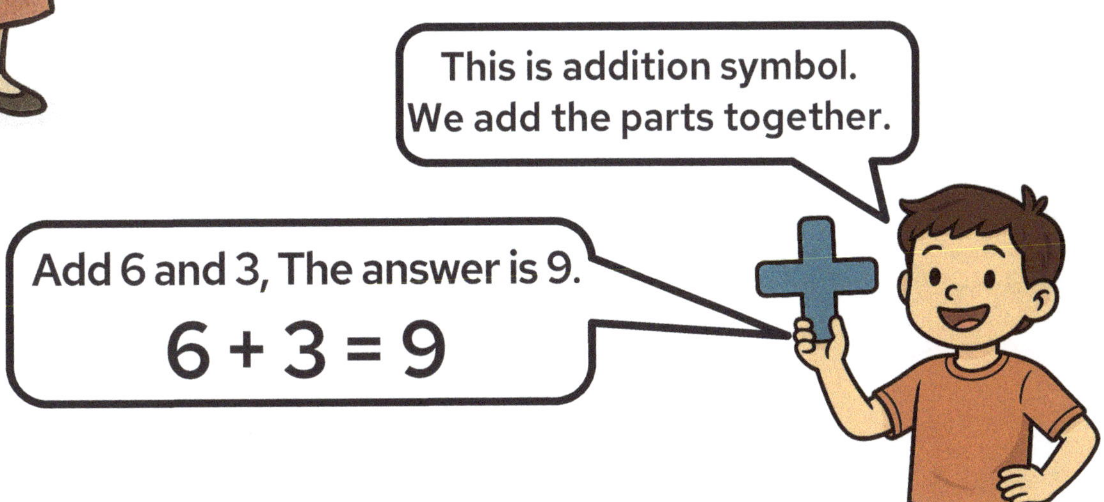

Here are 2 cars
Here are 3 bikes
Now we have 5 altogether

$2 + 3 = 5$

Here are 4 fishes
Here are 3 turtles
Now we have 7 altogether

$4 + 3 = 7$

5 friends are sitting.
5 friends are playing.
There are 10 friends altogether.

5 + 5 = 10

Here are 4 cats
Here are 6 kittens
Now we have 10 altogether

4 + 6 = 10

1. Look at each picture. Use the groups to make a story for the number sentence.

3 + 3 = 6

5 + 5 = 10

2 Learn Addition Using Number Bonds

4 + 3 = 7

3 + 4 = 7

2 + 1 = 3

1 + 2 = 3

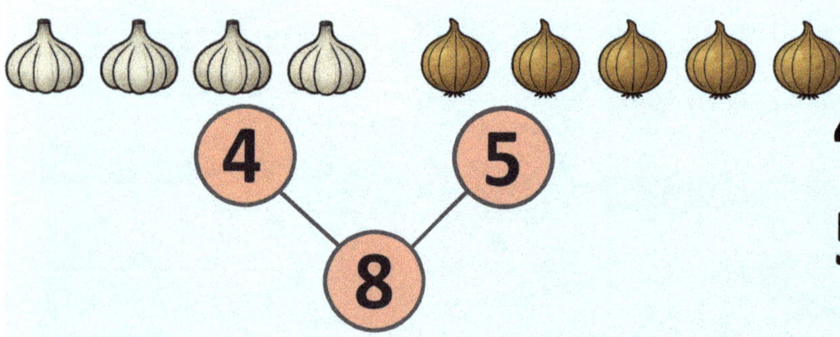

4 + 5 = 8

5 + 4 = 8

3 + 2 = 5

2 + 3 = 5

1. Count using number bonds

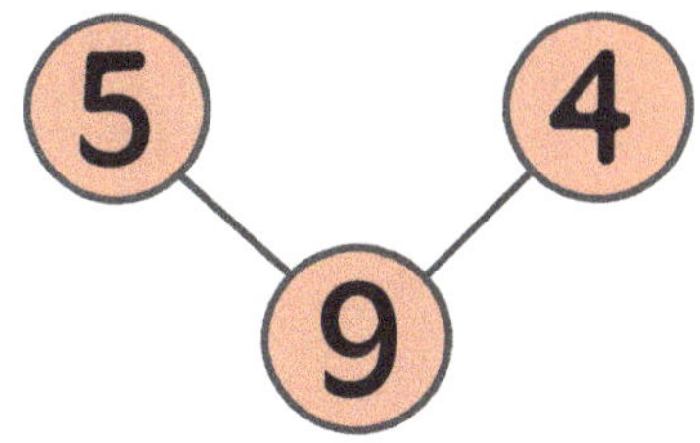

5 + 4 = 9

There are 9 fruits altogether

(a)

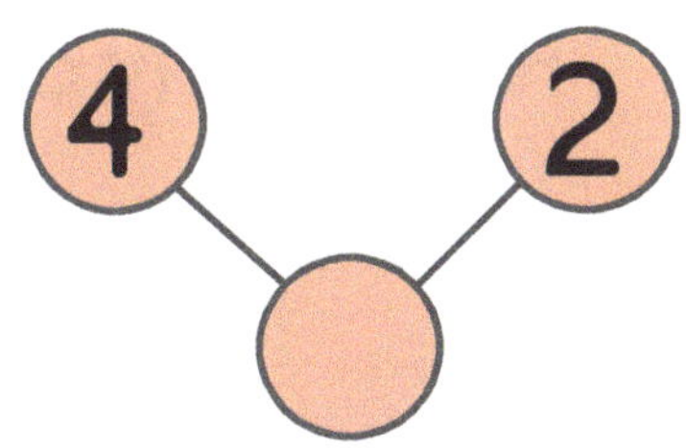

The boys are playing football in the field.
There are 4 boys playing in the front.
Then 2 more boys come to join them.

How many boys are there altogether?

4 + 2 =

(b)

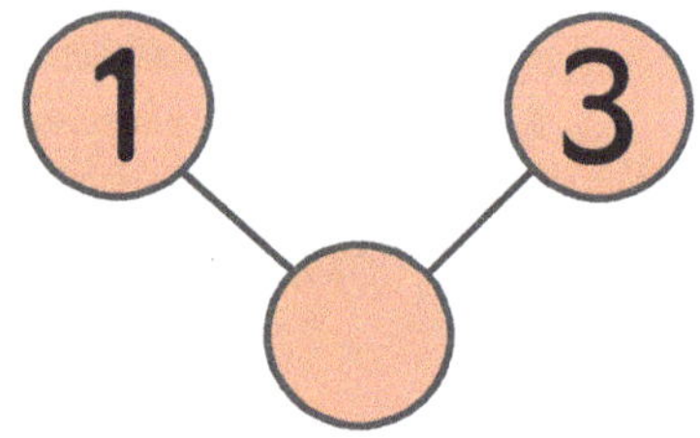

Benny has 1 carrot in his hand.

Then he finds 3 more carrots on the ground.

How many carrots does he have now:

$$1 + 3 = \square$$

(c)

There are 4 chocolate cookies on a plate.

Mom adds 2 strawberry cookies.

How many cookies are on the plate?

$$4 + 2 = \square$$

(d)

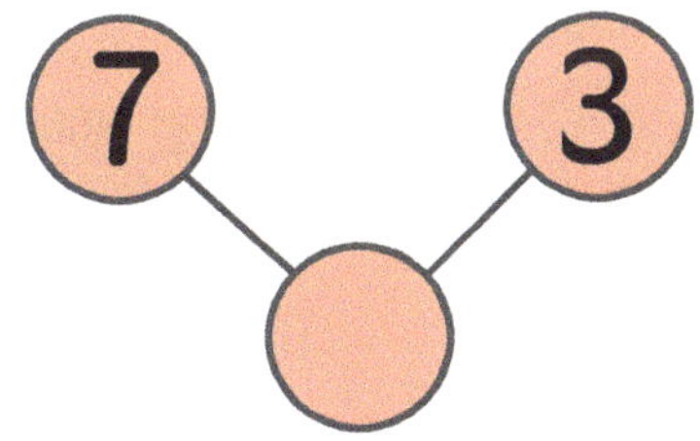

Penny catches 7 small fishes.
Later, she finds 3 bigger fishes in the water

How many fishes does she have now:

7 + 3 =

(e) Complete the below number sentences:

1 + 5 =

3 + 5 =

6 + 2 =

2 + 7 =

3 + 3 =

9 + 1 =

8 + 1 =

4 + 5 =

2.Count the red and blue pebbles. There are 10 pebbles altogether. Write the complete number sentence and the number bonds that make 10.

(a)

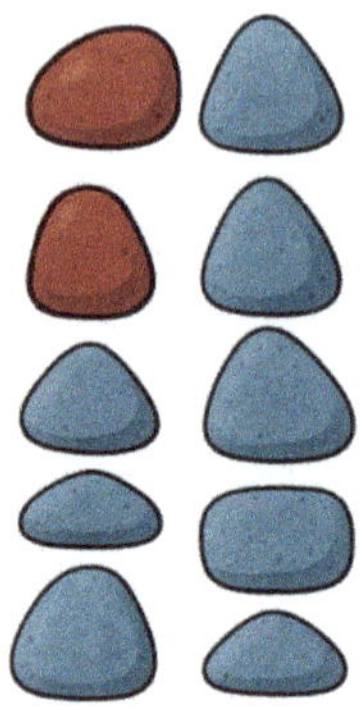

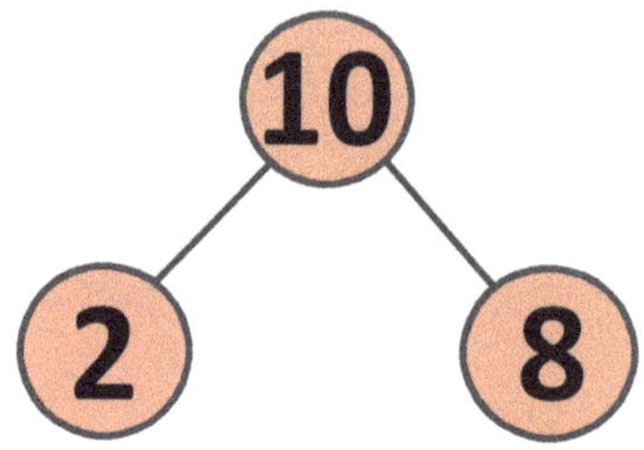

2 + 8 = 10

(b)

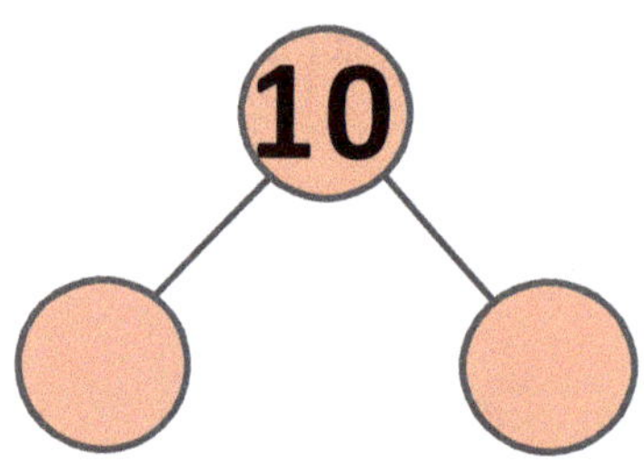

__ + __ = __

(c)

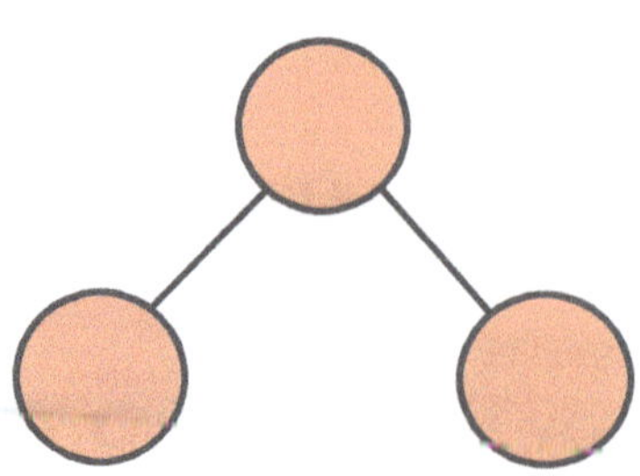

__ + __ = __

(d)

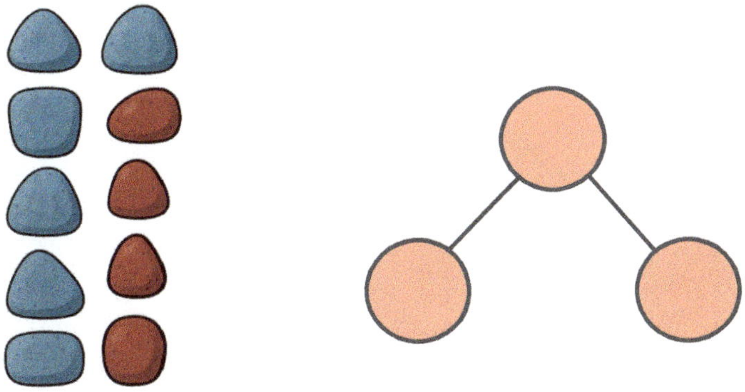

☐ + ☐ = ☐

(e)

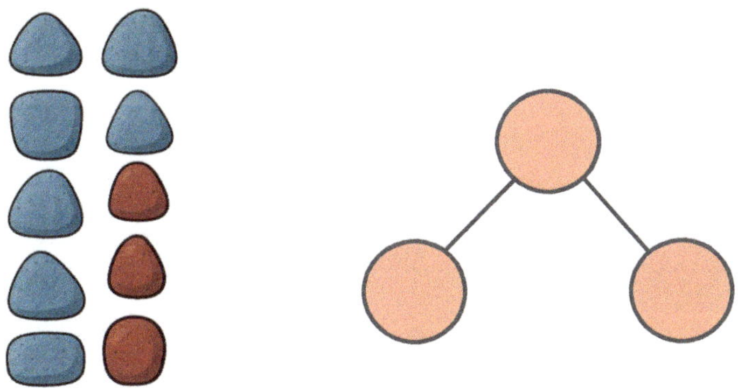

☐ + ☐ = ☐

(f)

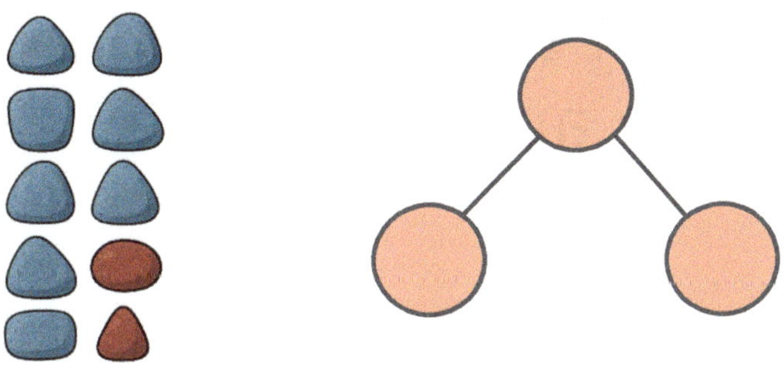

☐ + ☐ = ☐

(g)

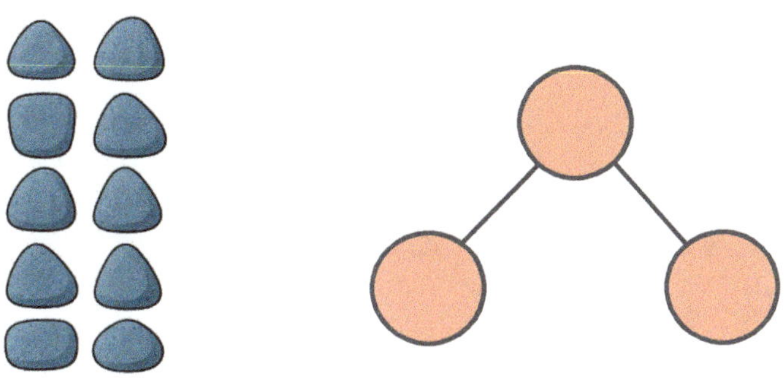

☐ + ☐ = ☐

3 Learn Addition by Adding More

Mina starts at 5 on the number line.
She wants to add 2 more.

She jumps 1 step forward to 6.
Then she jumps 1 more step to 7.

So, when we add 2 more:
5 + 2 = 7

1.Hop on the Number Line to Add More and Find the Number Sentences.

(a) Mina starts at 3 on the number line.

She hops **1 more** step forward.

Where does Mina land?

$$3 + 1 = \square$$

(b) Mina is standing at 2.

She wants **4 more**, so she jumps 4 steps to the right.

Which number does she reach?

$$2 + 4 = \square$$

(c) Mina is at 1 on the number line.

She hops **5 more** steps forward.

Where does she stay?

$$1 + 5 = \square$$

(d) Mina stands at 7.

She takes **2 more** steps forward.

Where does she stop?

$$7 + 2 = \square$$

Subtraction Within 10

1 Learn Subtraction with Fun Picture Stories!

There are 4 ice creams in the shop.

Raja takes 1 ice cream from the shop.

Now, there are 3 ice creams left.

When we take something away from a group, the number becomes smaller.

How to find the missing Baloon?

Riya is holding 5 colorful balloons in the park.

Suddenly, 1 baloon slips out of her hand.

She now has 4 balloons left.

$$5 - 4 = 1$$

When 1 balloon flies away, Riya has 1 less baloon.

Look at the pictures. After some apples fall,
how many apples are left on the tree?

A tree has 6 red apples.

2 apples fall down.

There are 6 apples on the tree. 2 apples fall down.
The number sentence is: **6 − 2 = 4**
So, **4** apples are left.

1.Look at the picture and fill in the number sentences.

(a) There are 6 fish swimming happily in the pond. A bird swoops down and takes 1 fish in its beak.Now, fewer fish are left in the pond.

How many fish are still in the water?

6 - 1 = ____

(b) There are 6 children on the beach. 2 children run away to play.

How many are left building sandcastles?

6 - 2 = ____

(c) Look at the picture.There are 5 cars on the road.
2 yellow cars move ahead.

How many green cars are left at the traffic signal?

5 - **2** = ☐

(d) There are 5 puppies. If 3 puppies run away,
How many puppies are left?

5 - **3** = ☐

(e) There are 7 flowers in the field. The children pick 3 flowers.

How many flowers are left growing in the field? Write the number sentence.

☐ - ☐ = ☐

(f) There are 7 little birds standing together on the grass.Suddenly, 1 bird flies away into the sky.

How many birds are left on the ground? Write the number sentence.

☐ - ☐ = ☐

2 Learn Subtraction Using Backward Counting

Backwards Counting: A Fun Way to Learn Subtraction!

Mina starts at **6**.
She jumps back **2** on the number line.

She jumps from **6 to 5**
and then She jumps to **4**.

Mina stops at **4**.

So, **6 - 2 = 4**

1. Hop Back on the Number Line to Subtract!

(a) Mina starts at 6 on the number line.
She hops 1 step backward.
Where does Mina land?

$$6 - 1 = \square$$

(b) Mina starts at 8 on the number line.
She hops 2 steps backward.
Where does Mina land?

$$8 - 2 = \square$$

(c) Mina starts at 7 on the number line.
She hops 3 steps backward.
Where does Mina land?

$$7 - 3 = \square$$

(d) Mina starts at 9 on the number line.
She hops 4 steps backward.
Where does Mina land?

$$9 - 4 = \square$$

3 Subtraction using Number Bonds

We start with a whole,we take away a part

The number bond helps us to find the missing part

Number Sentences

$$8 - 3 = 5$$

$$8 - 5 = 3$$

1. Look at each picture. Make a number bond and write the number sentences.

(a)

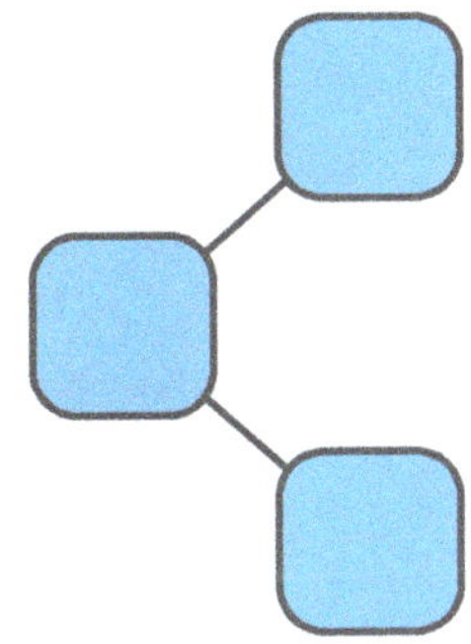

□ - □ = □ and □ - □ = □

(b)

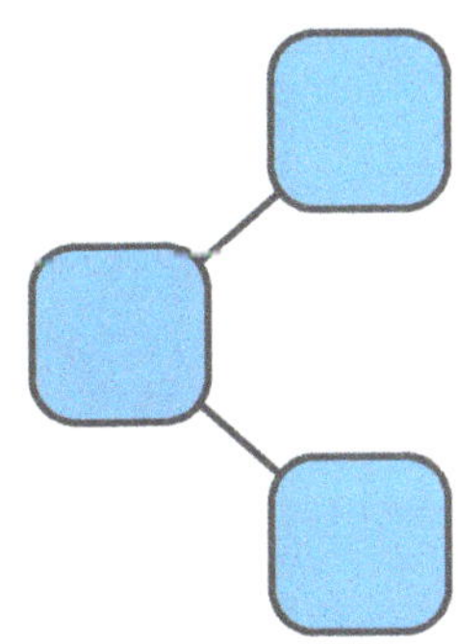

□ - □ = □ and □ - □ = □

(c)

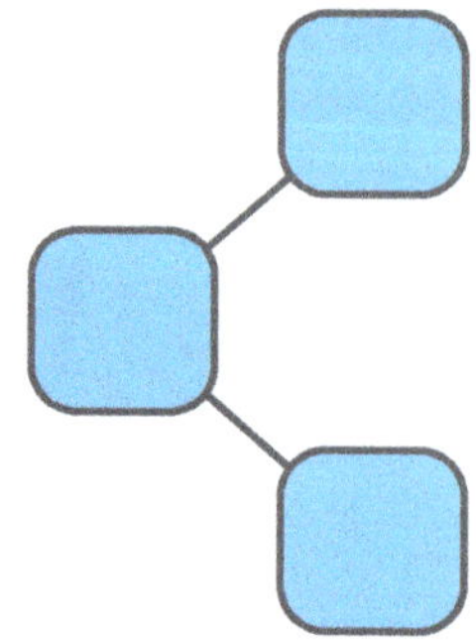

☐ - ☐ = ☐ and ☐ - ☐ = ☐

(d)

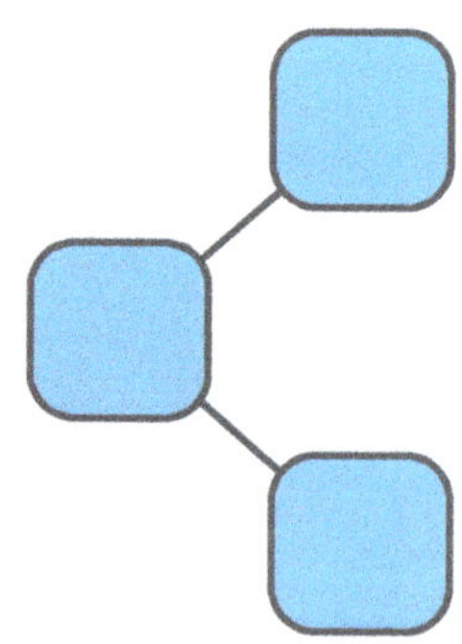

☐ - ☐ = ☐ and ☐ - ☐ = ☐

(e)

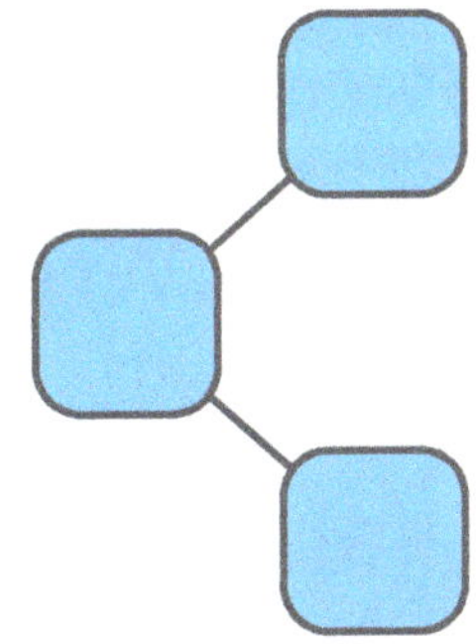

□ - □ = □ and □ - □ = □

(f)

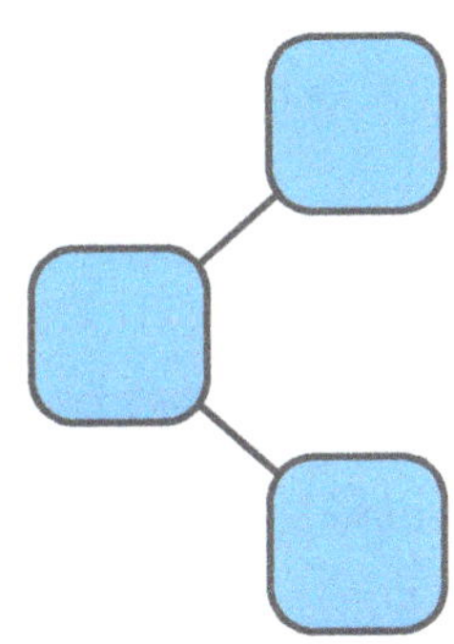

□ - □ = □ and □ - □ = □

2. Each picture shows a group of red and blue pebbles making a total of 10.

For each picture:

1. Construct the number bond for 10
2. Write two related subtraction sentences

(a)

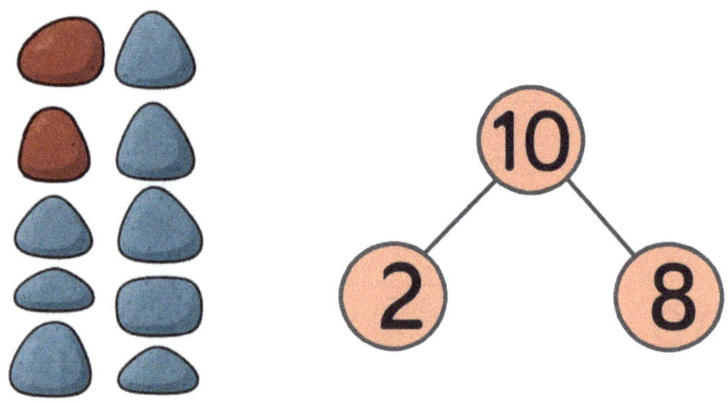

10 - 2 = 8

10 - 8 = 2

(b)

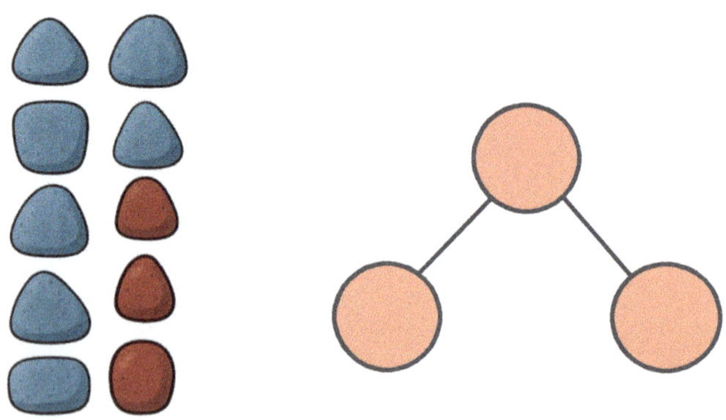

___ - ___ = ___

___ - ___ = ___

(c)

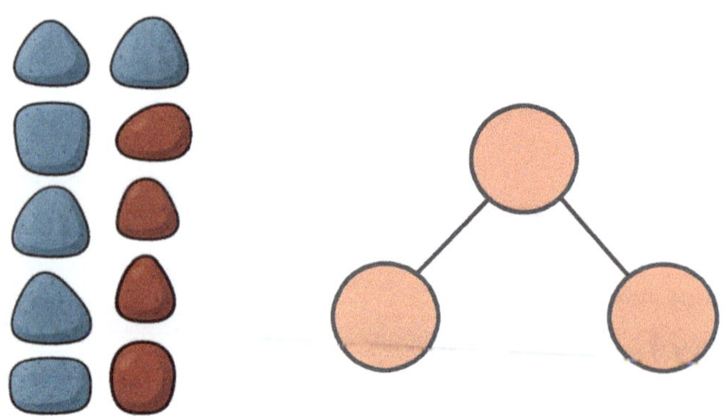

___ - ___ = ___

___ - ___ = ___

(d)

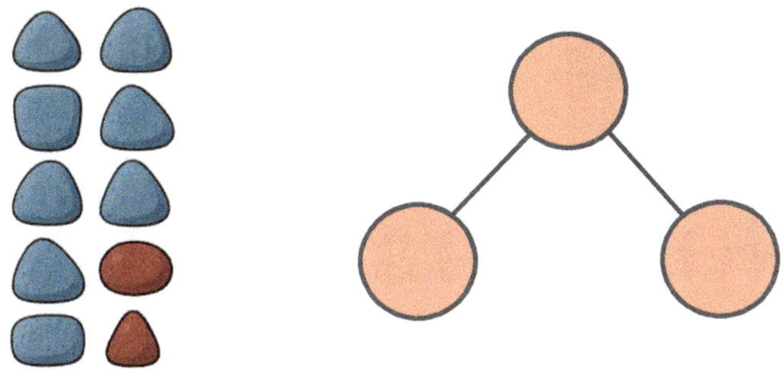

☐ - ☐ = ☐

☐ - ☐ = ☐

(e)

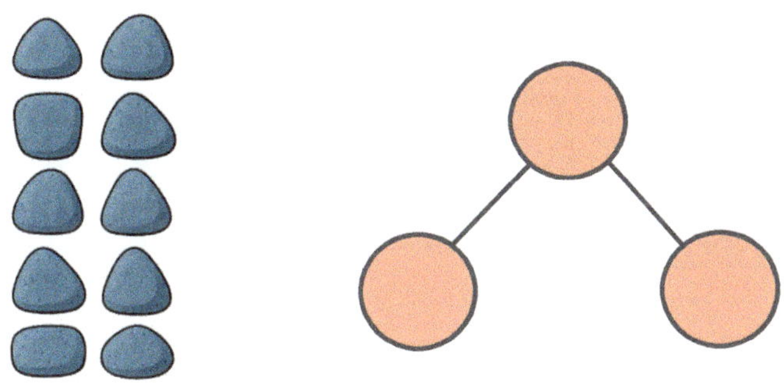

☐ - ☐ = ☐

☐ - ☐ = ☐

(f)

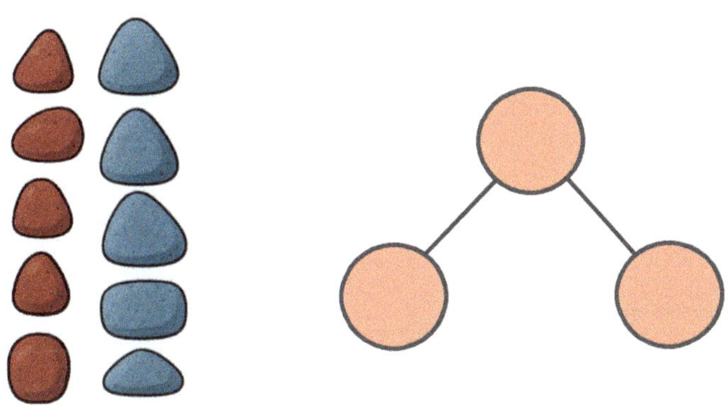

☐ - ☐ = ☐

☐ - ☐ = ☐

(g)

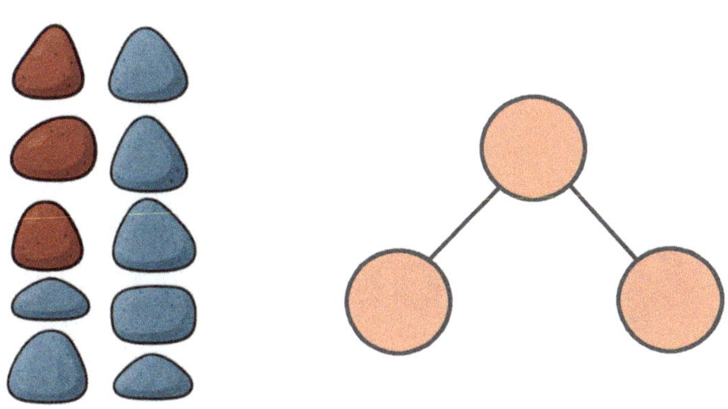

☐ - ☐ = ☐

☐ - ☐ = ☐

Learning Numbers to 20

1 Understanding Two-Digit Numbers 11 to 20

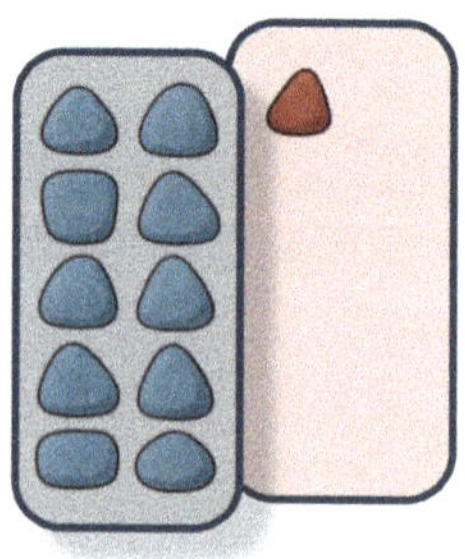

11 Eleven

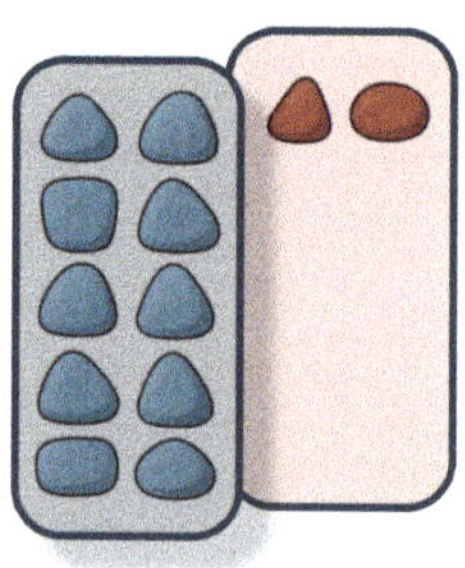

12 Twelve

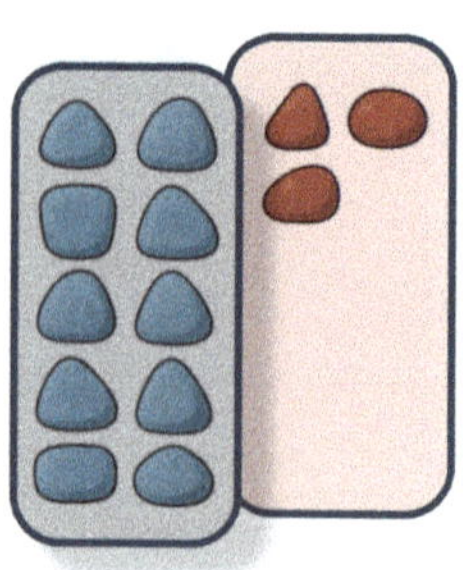

13 Thirteen

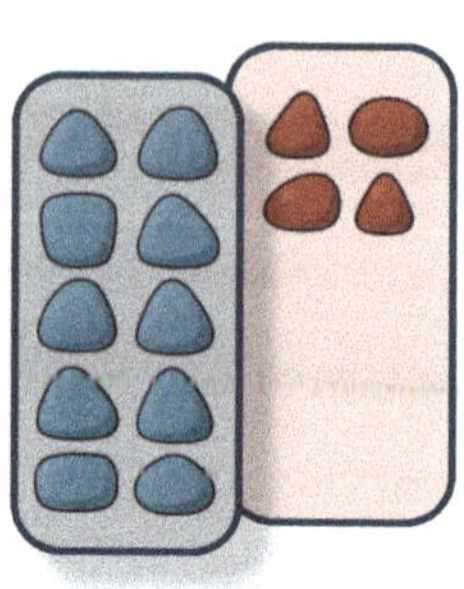

14 Fourteen

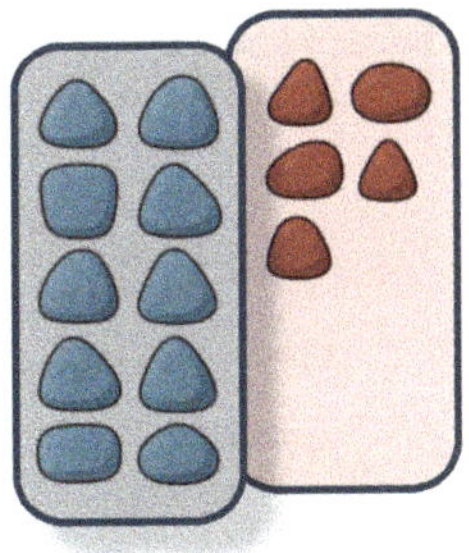

15 Fifteen

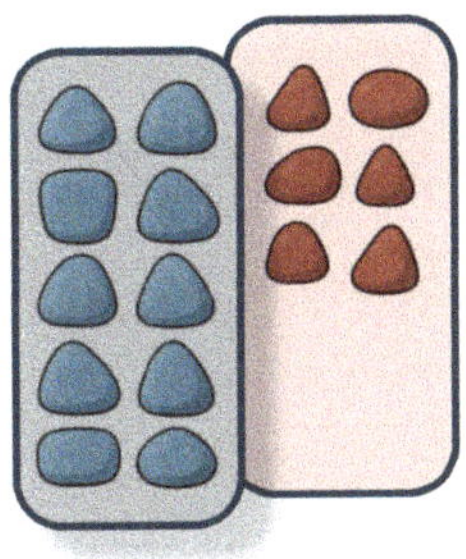

16 Sixteen

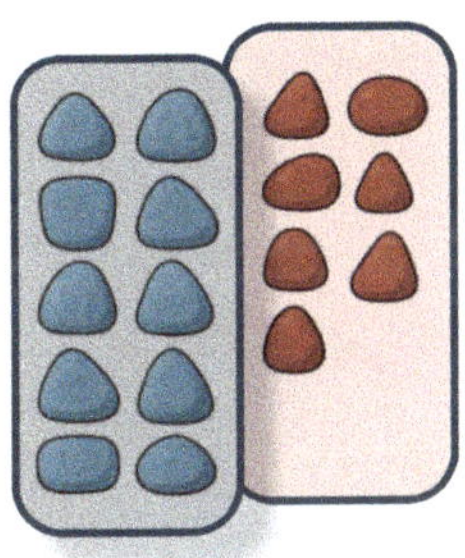

17 Seventeen

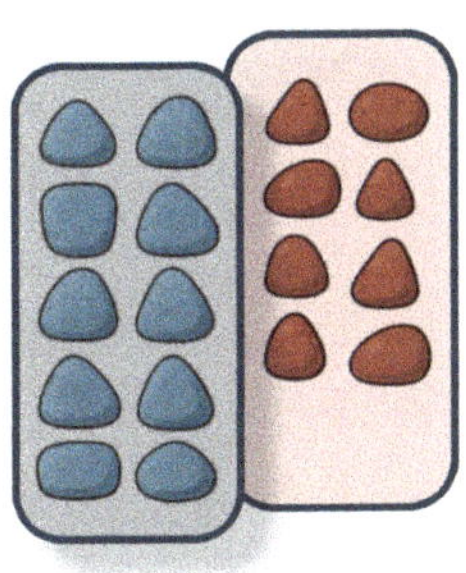

18 Eighteen

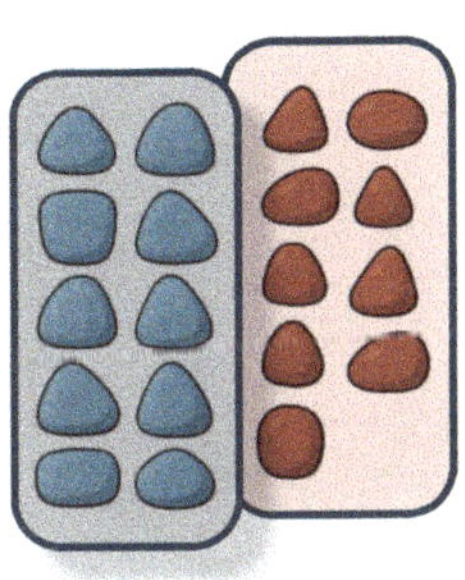

19 Nineteen

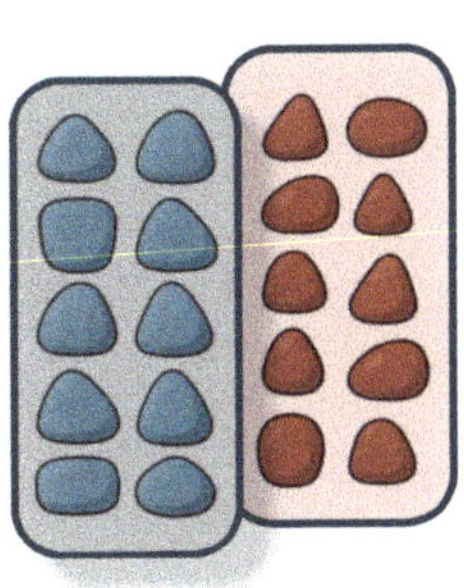

20 Twenty

1. Write the missing numbers inside the balloon

(a)

(b)

(c)

2. How many frogs are there?

☐ is 10 and 4

3. Circle 10 ladybirds, count the rest, and write the number sentence:

10 + ☐ = ☐

4. Which set has the greater number?

A

B

5. Which set has the smaller number?

A

B

6. Which set has the greatest number?
Which set has the smallest number?

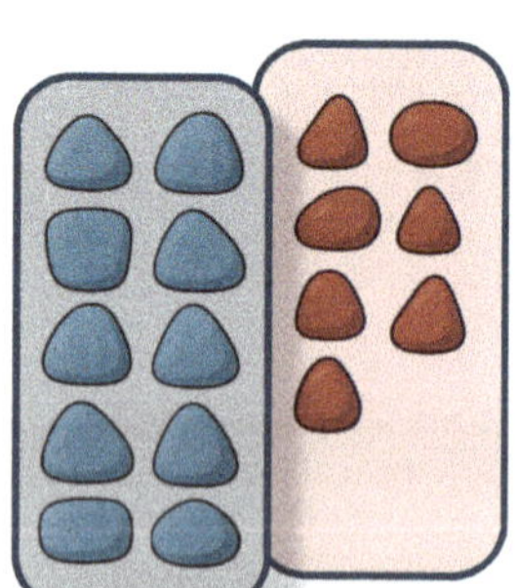

A

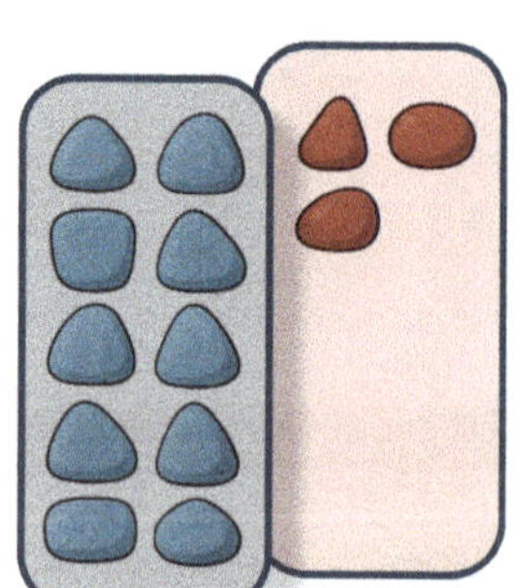

B

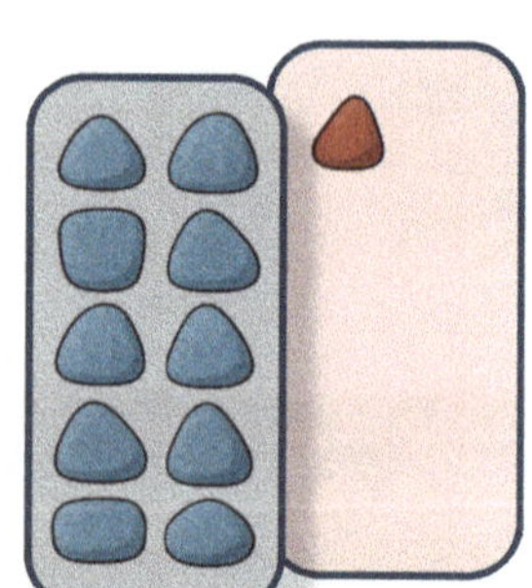

C

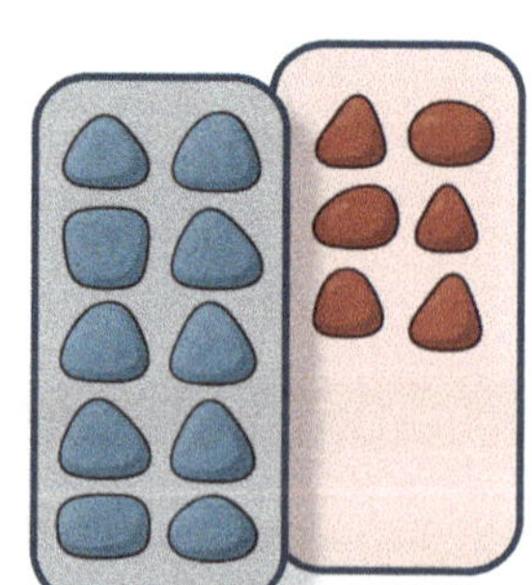

D

7. Which is greater 15 or 19?

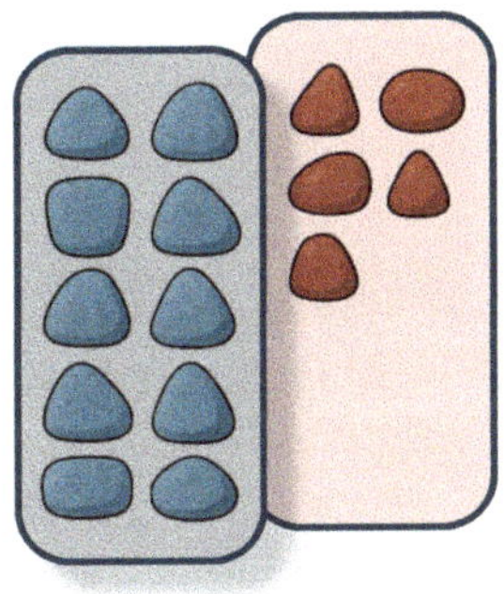 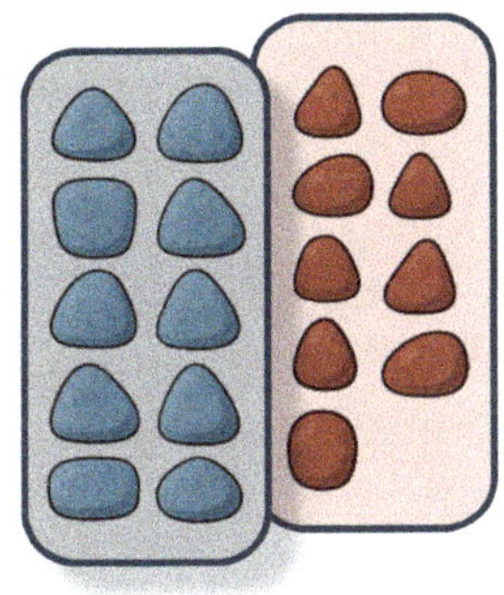

8. Which is smaller 13 or 16?

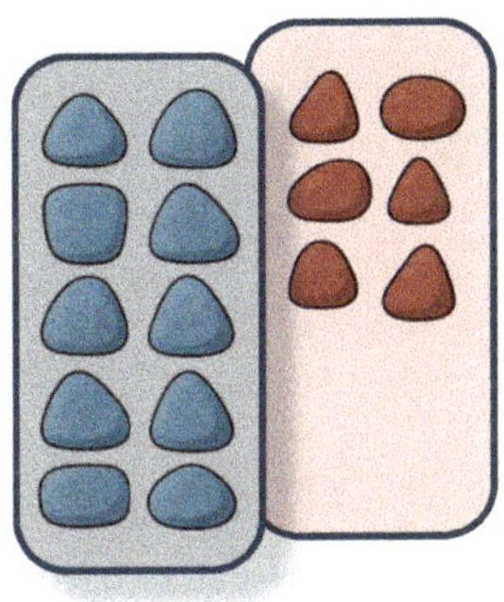 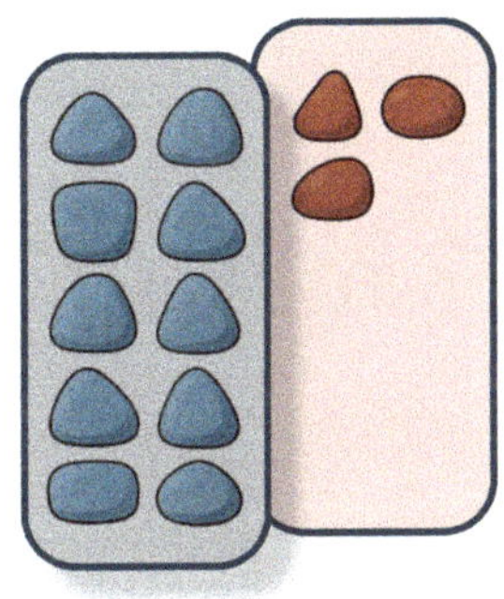

9. Compare the below numbers

15 8 18 12

Arrange the numbers in orders, Start with a smallest number.

Which number is greatest?

Which number is smallest?

10. From the pictures below, circle the group of ten and count the remaining objects.

(a)

10 Parrots

3Parrots

10 and 3 make **13**

10 + 3 = **13**

(b)

10 Pineapples

6 Pineapples

10 and 6 make ☐

10 + 6 = ☐

(c)

10 and 8 make ☐

10 + 8 = ☐

(d)

10 and 5 make ☐

10 + 5 = ☐

2 Addition with in 20

Add by making 10 first.

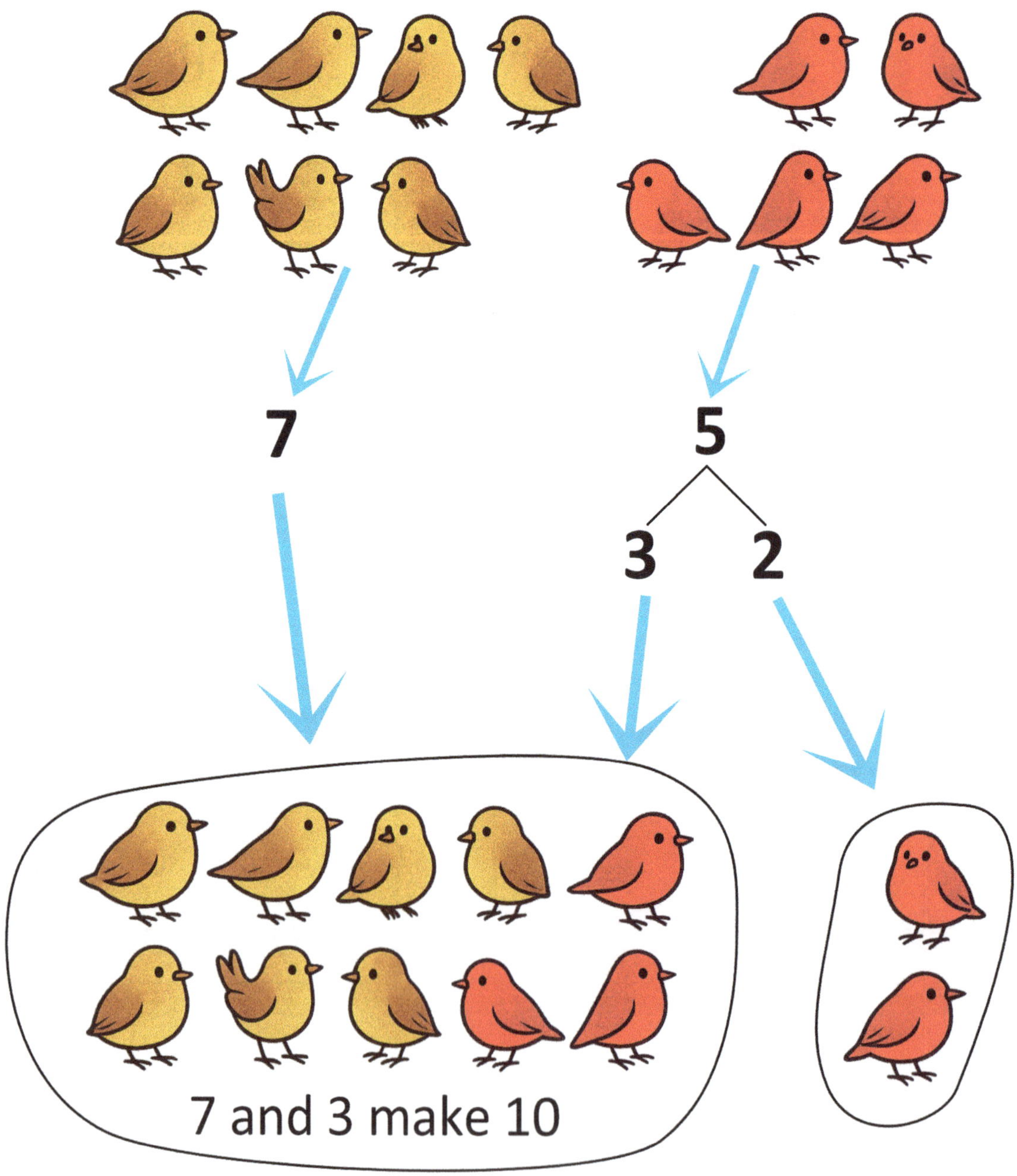

7 + 5 = 12

1. Look at the pictures below and write the addition sentences.

(a) How many apples altogether?

$$8 + 7 = ?$$

7

2 5

First step is make 10

$$8 + 7 = \square$$

There are $\square$ apples altogether.

2. Look at the picture stories and use the "make 10" method to count.

(a)

6 + 7

3 3

6 + 7 = ☐

(b)

9 + 7

1 6

9 + 7 = ☐

(c)

7 + 8

(7 splits into two boxes: ___ ___)

7 + 8 = ___

(d) Complete the below addition sentences.

2 + 5 = ___

9 + 7 = ___

7 + 3 = ___

8 + 9 = ___

2 + 6 = ___

4 + 8 = ___

5 + 5 = ___

9 + 9 = ___

1 + 9 = ___

5 + 6 = ___

3 Subtraction with in 20

Subtraction means we count backward.

If we start at 15 and take away 1, we go down one step to 14.

"Each step down means taking away 1."

15 → 14 → 13 → 12 → 11 → ...

"We count backward to find how many are left."

1. Find the subtraction sentence.

$$12 - 4 = ?$$

Count backward from 12.

11
10
9
8

From 12 to count backward 11, 10, 9, 8

$$12 - 4 = 8$$

5 - 2 = ☐	12 - 7 = ☐
4 - 3 = ☐	18 - 3 = ☐
5 - 2 = ☐	15 - 5 = ☐
7 - 3 = ☐	13 - 4 = ☐
8 - 2 = ☐	19 - 2 = ☐

Shapes and Patterns

1 Learn Basic Shapes

TRIANGLE

SQUARE

RECTANGLE

CIRCLE

PENTAGON

HEXAGON

HEPTAGON

OCTAGON

OVAL

DIAMOND

SEMICIRCLE

TRAPEZIUM

CRESCENT

STAR

HEART

DECAGON

1. Look at the pictures and answer the questions about the shapes.

(a) Let's count the shapes and write your answer in the boxes below.

(b) Count the shapes on the rocket. Write the numbers in the boxes.

ROCKET FROM SHAPES

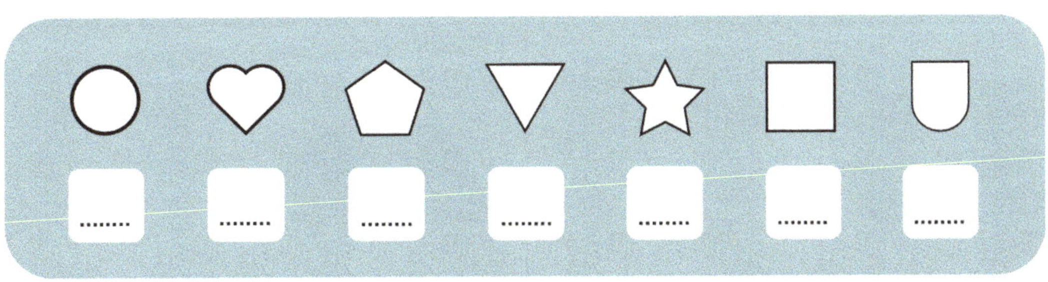

(c) Look at the shape pictures and ✓ the correct words

	RECTANGLE TRIANGLE
	SQUARE RECTANGLE
	SQUARE RECTANGLE
	PENTAGON HEPTAGON
	HEXAGON HEPTAGON
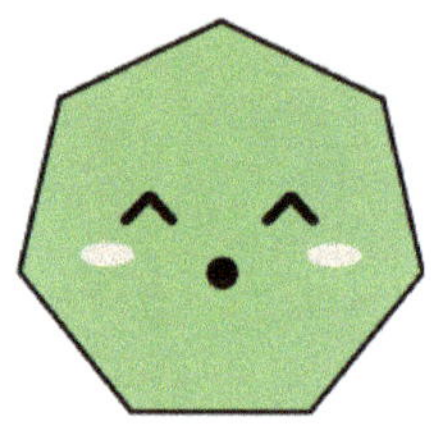	OCTAGON HEPTAGON
	OCTAGON TRAPEZIUM
	CIRCLE OVAL
	SEMICIRCLE OVAL
	SEMICIRCLE OVAL

(d) Match the shapes. Draw a line from the object on the left to theshape that matches it.

(e) Circle all the objects that have a trainngle face.

(f) Put a ✔ under the objects that are square.

(d) Match the shapes. Draw a line from the object on the left to theshape that matches it.

(e) Circle all the objects that have a trainngle face.

(f) Put a ✔ under the objects that are square.

(g) Compare the objects with the given shape:

CIRCLE

Which of these objects have a circle face?

Draw a ✓ under the objects that match the circle.

(h) Join the correct slices to complete the shape.

Slice Matching

- Let's match the slices below.

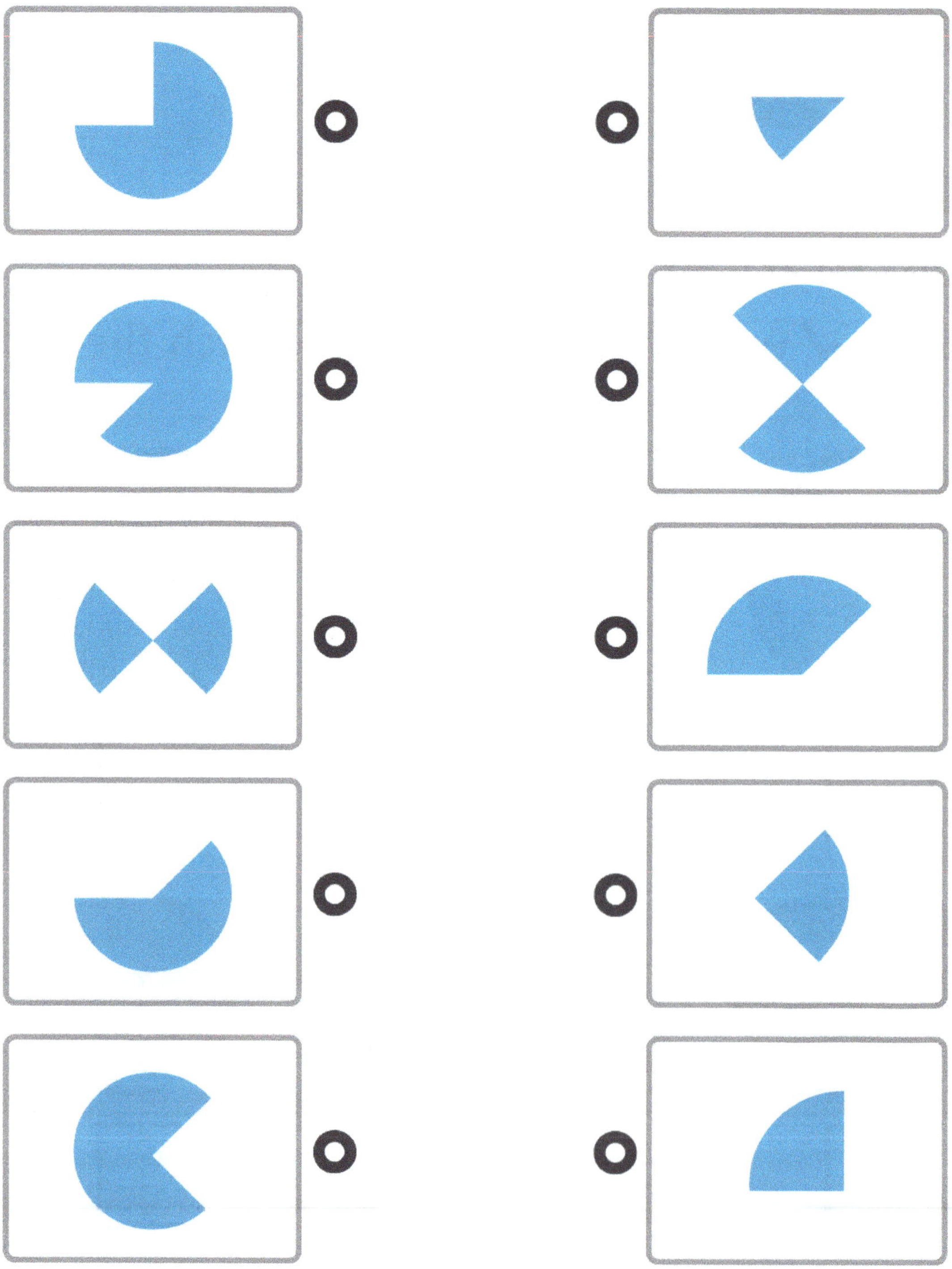

(i) Observe each pattern, identify the repeating sequence, and complete it by coloring the remaining shapes.

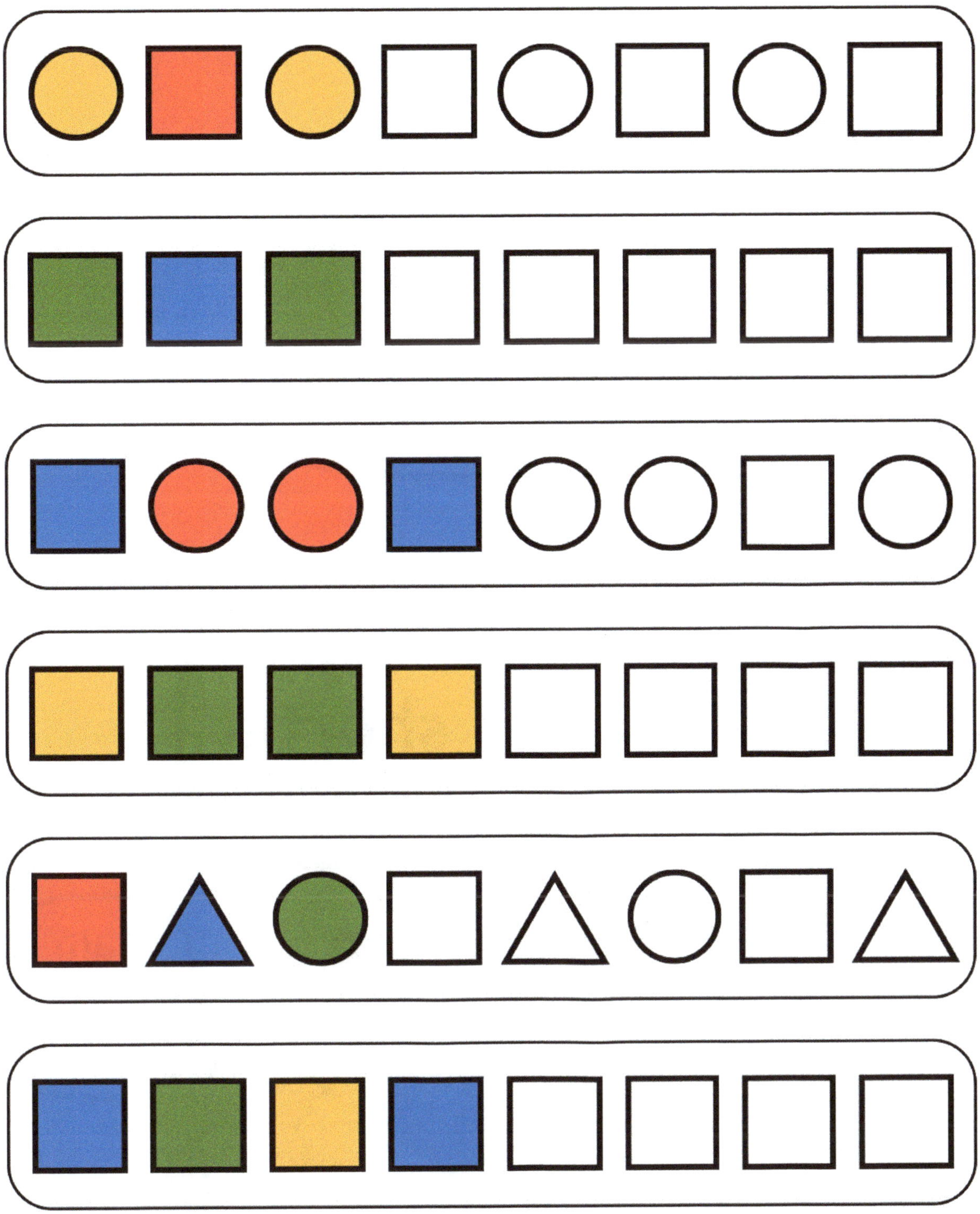

8

Length

1 Understanding Length
Longer, Shorter

1. Look at the pictures. Identify the tallest and the shortest.

(a) Which is the tallest tree?
Which is the shortest tree?

(b) Which one is the longest?
Which one is the shortest?

(c) Look at the picture and compare animals.

LION GIRAFFE HIPPO ELEPHANT

(1) Which one is the shortest animal ____________.

(2) Which one is the tallest animal ____________.

(3) Which one is the second tallest animal ____________.

(4) Which one is the third tallest animal ____________.

2 Fun ways to Measure

What is a Unit?

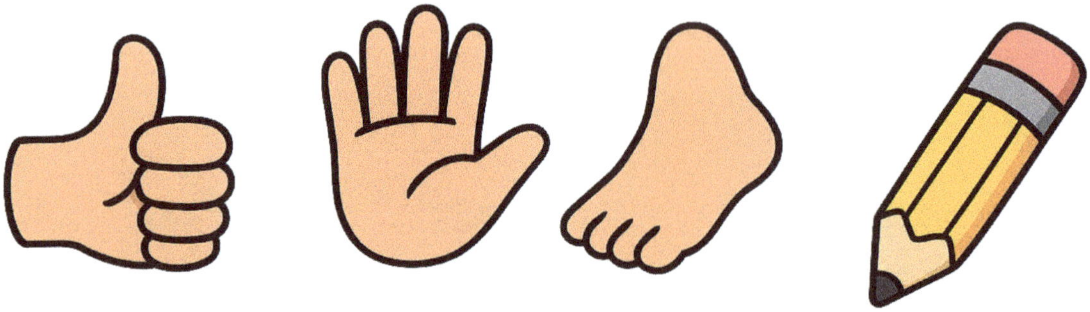

A unit is anything we use to measure length, like a thumb, palm, foot, or pencil.

Measuring with a Pencil

4 pencils long

(c) Look at the picture and compare animals.

LION GIRAFFE HIPPO ELEPHANT

(1) Which one is the shortest animal ____________.

(2) Which one is the tallest animal ____________.

(3) Which one is the second tallest animal ____________.

(4) Which one is the third tallest animal ____________.

2 Fun ways to Measure

What is a Unit?

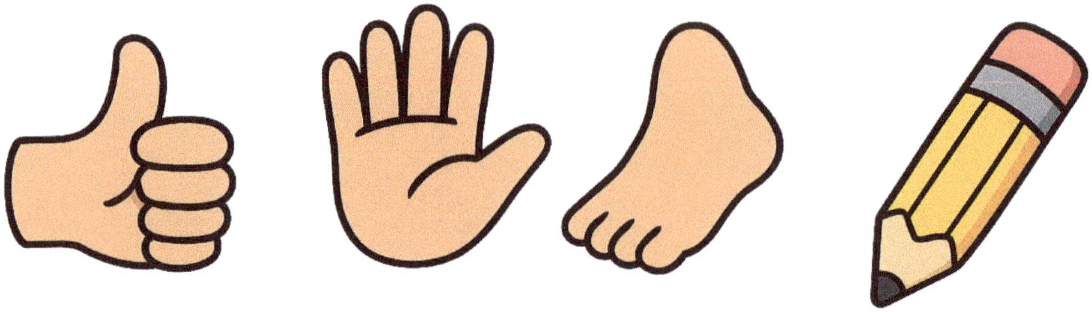

A unit is anything we use to measure length, like a thumb, palm, foot, or pencil.

Measuring with a Pencil

4 pencils long

Measuring with My Palm

Measuring with My Foot

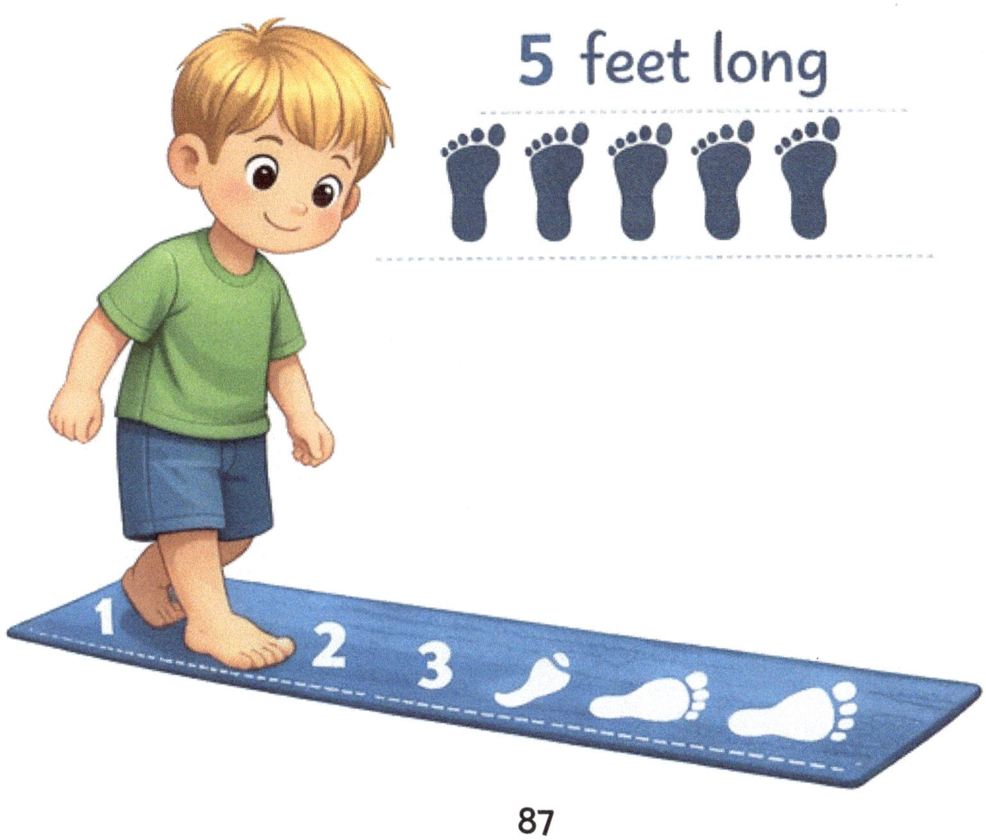

1.Fun Ways to Measure Length

(a) Measure Your Table!

Task:

- Take your pencil.
- Use it to measure the length of your table.

My table is ☐ pencils long.

(b) Measure your Pencil using Eraser!

Task:

- Take your eraser.
- Place the eraser next to the pencil and measure its length.
- Count how many erasers long the pencil is.
- Write the number in the box.

My pencil is ☐ erasers long.

(c) Measure your Own Book!

- Take your own book.
- Use your palm to measure its length.
- Count how many palms long it is.

My book is ☐ palms long.

(d) Measure your Room!

Task:

- Walk across your room starting from a wall.
- Use your own feet to measure the length of your room.

My room is ☐ feet long.

9 Weight

The toy box is **heavier**. The teddy is **lighter**.

Which is the **lightest**?

Which is the **heaviest**?

1 Understanding weight : Heavy, Light

The heavy school bag goes down.
The light book goes up.

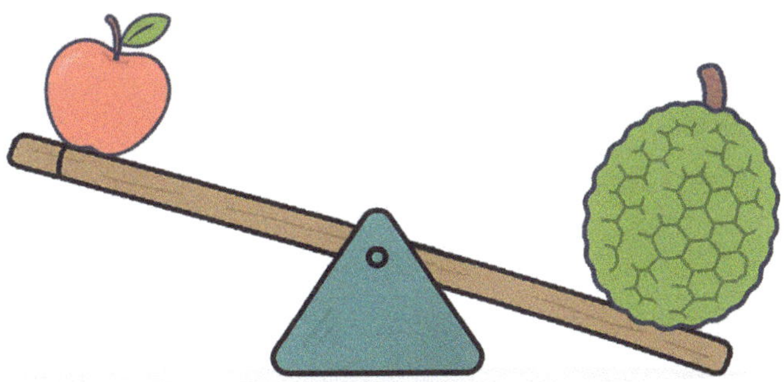

The jackfruit is heavier than apple.
The apple is lighter than jackfruit.

Which is heavier?
Which is lighter?

1. Circle the object that weighs heavier than the other.

a.  

b.  

c.  

d.  

2 Measuring weight using simple units

How Heavy Is Your Tiffin Box?

Maya uses crayons to measure weight.
Each spoon = 1 unit.

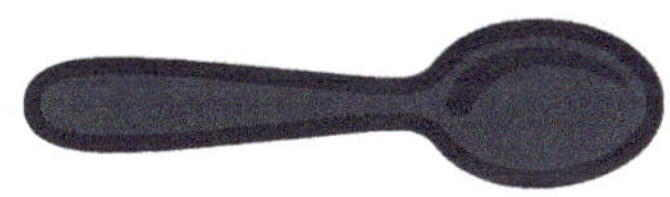

Maya wants to measure the weight of her empty tiffin box.

The water bottle is ☐ spoons heavy.

www.ingramcontent.com/pod-product-compliance
Ingram Content Group UK Ltd.
Pitfield, Milton Keynes, MK11 3LW, UK
UKHW061550190726
13845UKWH00030B/1101

9 789356 267732